Drawing Scorpions
How to Draw Scorpions
For the Beginner

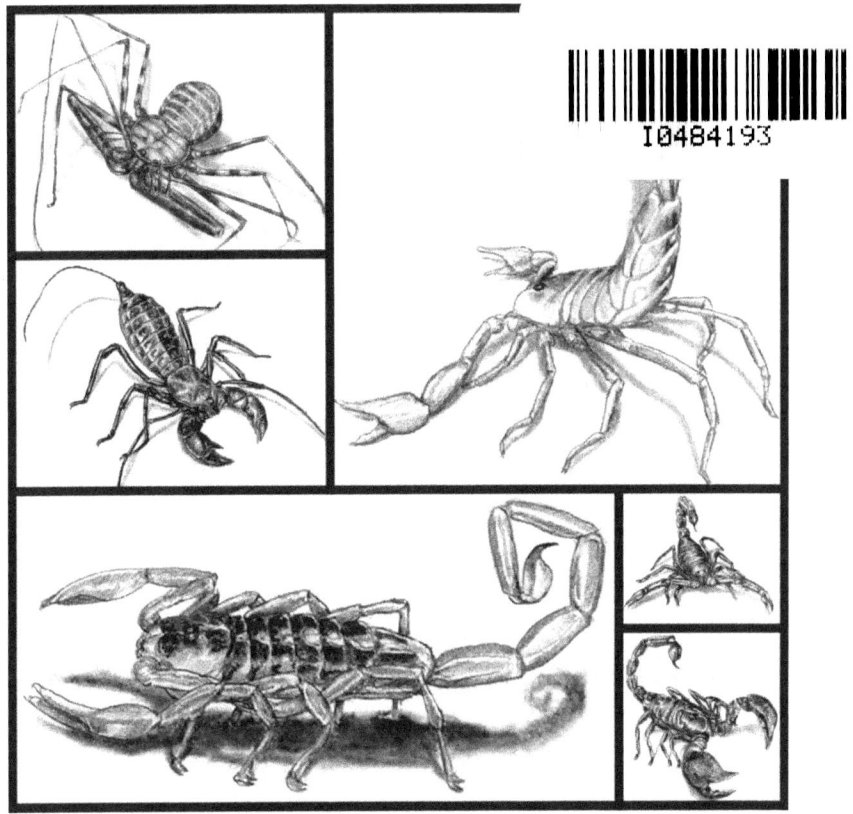

Adrian Sanqui
And
John Davidson

Learn to Draw Series
Mendon Cottage Books
JD- Biz Publishing

All Images Licensed
By: Adrian Sanqui, Paolo Lopez de Leon, Fotolia and 123rf

Learn How to Draw Books for the Absolute Beginner

TABLE OF CONTENTS

Drawing tools

Pencils

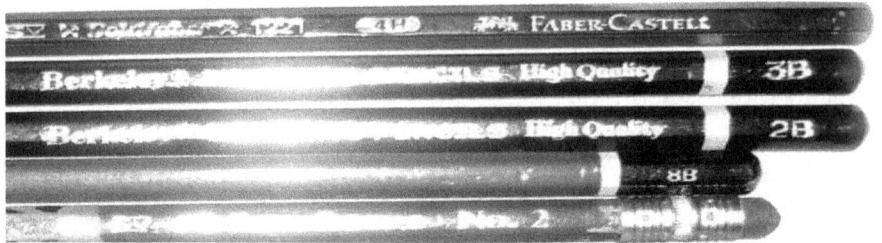

The most important tool you need to be able to enhance your drawing skills is a medium that can be corrected if you made some sloppy line strokes. Knowing and using more than just one type of pencil is a big help and it is better if you have pencils of different grades so you can easily produce the kind of lightness or darkness you want to make. The 'H' engraved near the pencil's tip (side of eraser) stands for "hardness" and it ranges from 2H to 9H. A pencil with only an "H" mark and doesn't have a number means 1H. The most common type (the one available anywhere) of pencil that does not indicate its grade mark is usually a 2H pencil. The "B" marking of pencils stand for "blackness", this means that they can easily produce darker line marks and are softer than H pencils. It ranges from HB (hard and dark) to 9B (very soft and very dark), so when it comes to B pencils, the higher the number is; the softer and darker it becomes. Different brands have different softness, hardness and blackness levels, so if you are going to use a certain brand for the first time, you should try them out first before applying it on your main drawing.

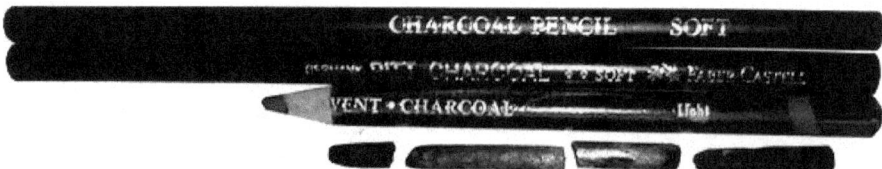

Charcoal pencils also come in different grades. The generic grades of soft, medium and hard are available in different brands. Charcoal pencils are a bit messy to work with; even the 'hard' grade charcoal pencil is still relatively softer compared to those with 4B to 6B grade pencils. It is most advisable for drawings that would require a lot of smeared shading for a smoother and wider portrayal of gradation.

Mechanical pencil

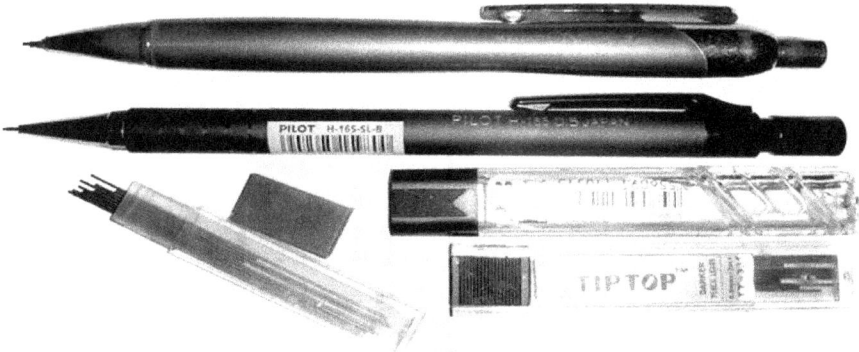

A mechanical pencil has a consistent wick or point which makes it easier for you to maintain the thickness of the line marks you produce. Mechanical pencils are good for small and subtle detailing that requires very thin lines, instead of sharpening your pencil several times just to have a thin and constant fine point that you need. Different grades of lead or graphite is also available for refilling your mechanical pencil, just make sure that the size of the point your pencil has is also the same as the pencil leads you refill it with. They come in several sizes and style, but what really matters is it does what it's supposed to.

Sharpener

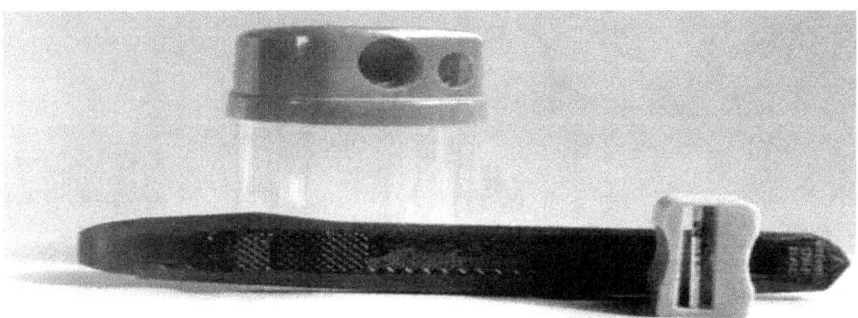

A regular sharpener is quite dependable if you are using H and low B pencils, but if you are going to use it to sharpen a pencil with very soft graphite cores then it may keep on breaking, most especially if you will use it for a charcoal lead pencil. A good substitute for regular sharpeners is a cutter, so you can easily control the pressure that should just be enough to expose the core and achieve a fine point. Cutters are often used if you want a "chisel" point pencil that is very helpful for thick and thin linings.

Erasers

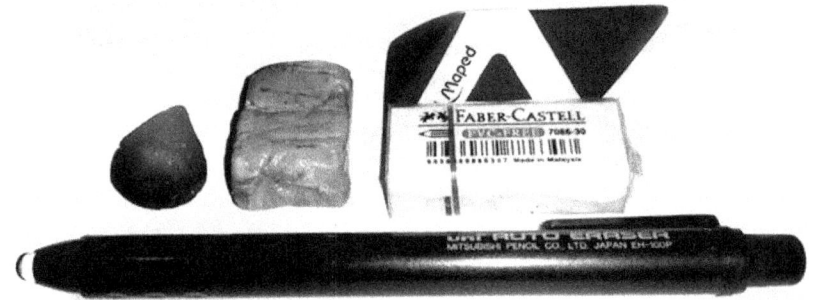

Pencils are no good if you don't have a good quality eraser, having an eraser is essential if you are going to use a pencil for drawing. Choose a rubber eraser that is soft and not the ones that leave a faint color or worst is a scratch on the paper. Don't leave your eraser lying around on the table or just anywhere, keep it on a pencil case or anything that can protect it from being exposed on air for too long because some erasers (cheaper ones) harden when it's left lying around because it will dry out and harden.

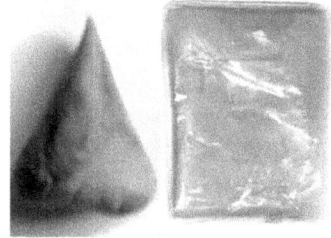

A kneadable eraser is very helpful for making highlights and reaching hardly accessible areas such as the gloss on the eyes or light portions of fingernails and such. It usually looks like a gray slab or a small bar of clay that can be molded or deformed to any shape you desire. It doesn't rub off the marking like usual erasers, but instead, it lifts off the graphite from the paper, like absorbing it. Instead of rubbing the eraser with a certain pressure to remove a marking, carefully dab on the portions you want to erase or to simply decrease the applied graphite or charcoal until you recover the brightness (whiteness of the paper) you want. Kneaded erasers can still be useful as long as they aren't already too dirty or dry. Keep it in a concealed container to lengthen its usefulness, because just like how good it is for absorbing graphite, it would also easily catch dust.

Smudge
sticks

A smudge stick is used for smearing the shades on the portions that are hard to access. Some artists dull down the other tip so it can be used for distributing the shades on the big areas. To avoid ruining the smudge stick, use a sand paper to make a blunter tip or to make it even pointier. Smudge sticks or blending stumps comes in different sizes, choose what best fits your needs and it will be a big help for blending gradations. Smudge sticks are cheap and are available on art stores. Common smudge sticks are just rolled and compressed hard papers, so try not to get it wet.

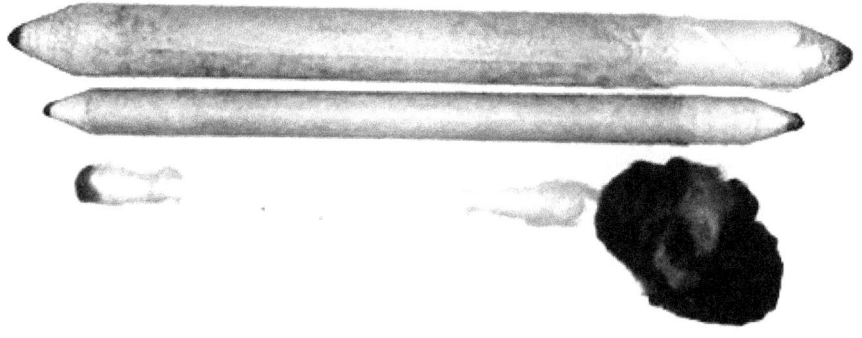

Keep those used up smudge sticks even if it's already in a rugged state (dirty or worn out), you never know when it might get handy. Dirty smudge sticks are useful for producing faint shades, and those with torn up tips can make textures that you might find useful.

If ever you cannot find a smudge stick available (although, I doubt this would be a problem if you have art stores near you, and if not, you can just order online. It is quite cheap) you can just make a tortillion for a temporary smudging tool (some artists actually prefer this one instead of smudge sticks). Use a thick piece of paper (like those on sketch pads, preferably the ones for watercolor drawings. Do not use thin and shiny papers). Fold it on one side and roll it up to create a cone, with the folded side at the tip.

Coloring materials

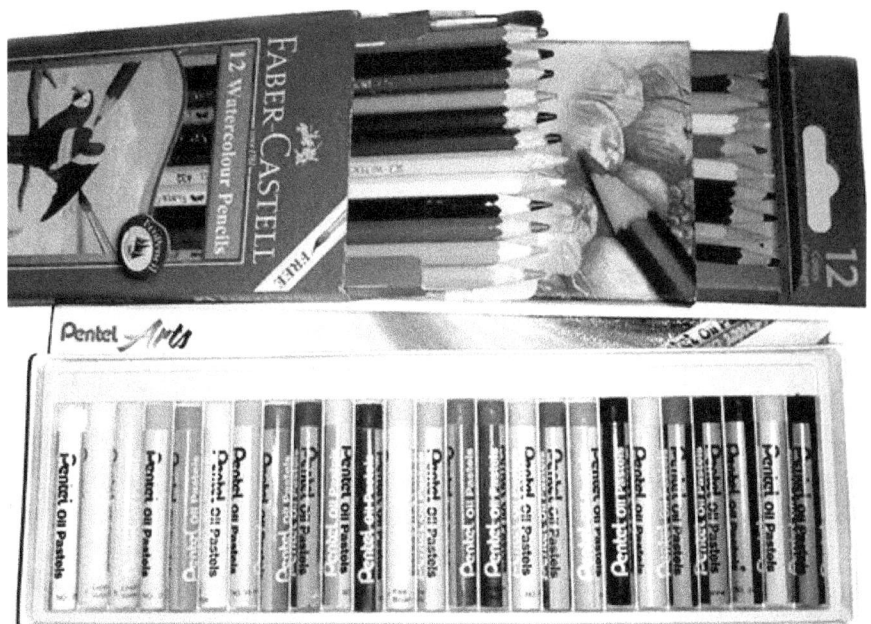

If you are planning to color your drawing, choose a coloring tool that best fits your needs.

Oil pastels are good for blending and synchronizing different colors together. It might get messy on your first trials (if you don't want to get messy, just place a clean piece of paper for your palm rest, to avoid rubbing your palm against the colored portions of your drawing) but you'll get the hang of it as you use it more often. Oil pastels are good for beginners as a practicing tool for smearing different color values.

Color pencils are the next best thing for filling your drawing with colored hatches (linear shading), or even coloring via scribbling. This coloring tool is best for small-sized illustrations. Although, the peak of the tone values that a common color pencil set can produce are far weaker than the oil pastel's, and it cannot be smeared (but there are available color pencils which can produce strong color tones just like oil pastel's or even acrylic's, but they are quite pricy; like the prisma color pencils).

This coloring tool is also a good practicing medium for beginners, and my personal favorite for quick colored sketches or even for illustrations with fairly detailed line work.

Parts of a Scorpion

It is much easier to draw a scorpion if you are familiar with its parts. In this way, you know which parts to include to properly compose the structure of a scorpion's figure.

If you are familiar with the basic parts of a scorpion, then you can easily draw one even without a model or picture to base upon. Just remember that aside from the color, size and few certain features, each kind of scorpions have certain differences in their body characteristics and that is how they are categorized.

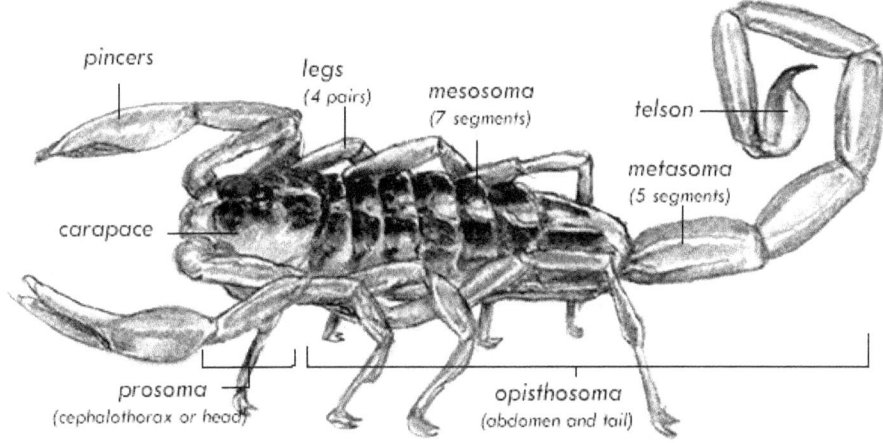

A scorpion has three basic body divisions:

The head which is also called prosoma (Cephalothorax) is covered or protected by the exoskeleton called carapace. The carapace has a slight dent on the top center where the median eyes are located. Depending on the species, the eyes on the front edges have two to five pairs.

Following right below the eye sets are the arms or the claws/pincers, which is also called pedipalps. The pedipalps have two parts; the upper claw which is called manus is fixed, while the lower claw or tarsus can be moved. Its jaws or mouth which is also called chelicerae is leveled at the center right below its arms.

The abdomen which is also called mesosoma contains 7 segments; they are easily distinguishable in dorsal view (back side) because of the exoskeleton (like armor plating) which is called sclerotosed plate. Although in ventral view, (underside) only 4 plates are observable, (scorpions are less-likely to be drawn ventrally) they contain a pair of short slits (like air holes which is called book lungs) called spiracles, positioned diagonally on the sides of each ventral segments. The sclerotosed gradually increase in width (coming from the head and down to the tail).

The tail of the scorpion which is also called metasoma contains five segments excluding the segment of the stinger or the telson. The segments of the tails gradually become longer (from the abdomen and down) as it reach the stinger. The telson that is in shape of a teardrop has two parts; the venom gland or the vesicle, and the slightly curved pointed tip which is called aculeus.

A scorpion has four pair of legs (eight limbs) with pointy feet (coxa), each pair with slightly different length, with the first pair as the shortest and the last pair as the longest. These legs are all located right beneath the prosoma (ventral view), with the first pair located right next to the arms/pincers.

Body Posture

The body of a scorpion has fairly limited bending capability and positions. Each of its parts has limited movements. The abdomen of a scorpion can hardly curve sideward, but it can easily bend upwards. The limbs (legs and arms) are quite graceful, most especially the legs. The legs can almost overlap one another when the scorpion is crawling. The tail is the most flexible portion of the scorpion's body, it can arc sideward and forward in different manners and degrees.

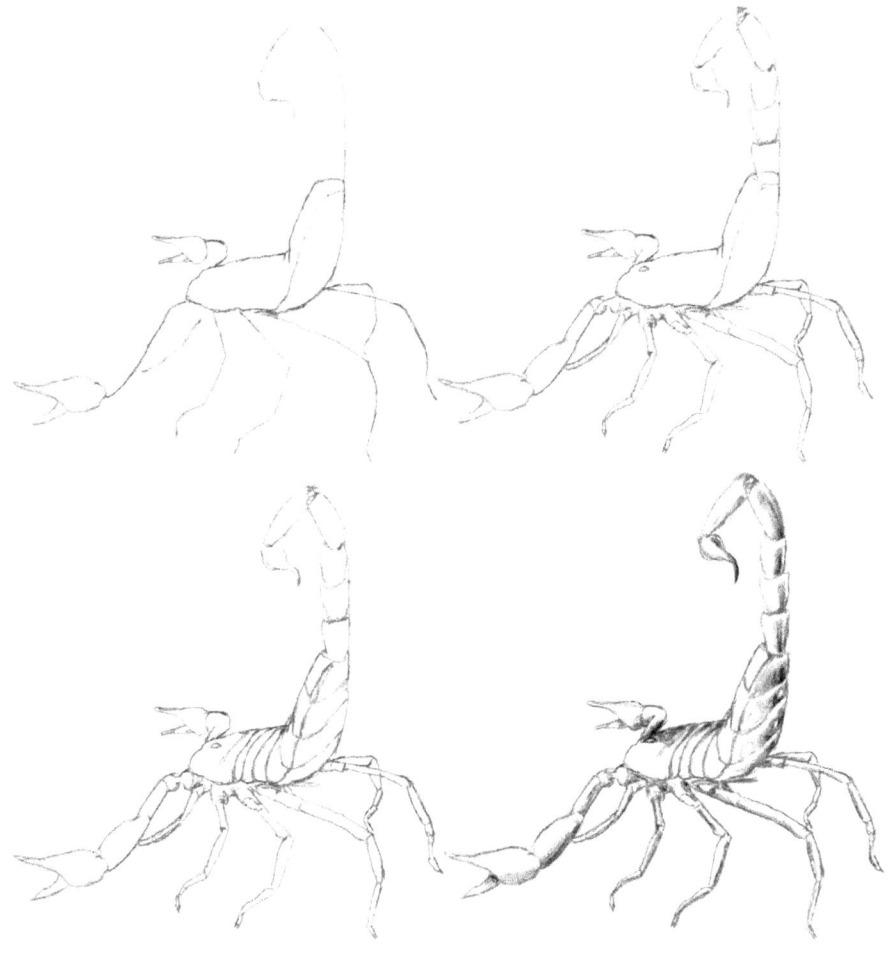

When a scorpion is about to attack (aiming its stinger) or in a defensive stance, its tail is arced forward (noticeably more bent than usual), or stiffened in an inverted 'J' shape, and the arms are often posed in a 'C' position. Its claws are open as it closely observes its enemy/prey as it tracks its next move. And when it attacks, it raises the lower portion of its body (almost straightening and stiffening the segments on its last pair legs in a right angle) to further extend the reach of its tail so it could sting the target even if it fails to hold it down. Scorpions usually grab their targets by the limbs so they can pull them closer and then aim for the head or the body.

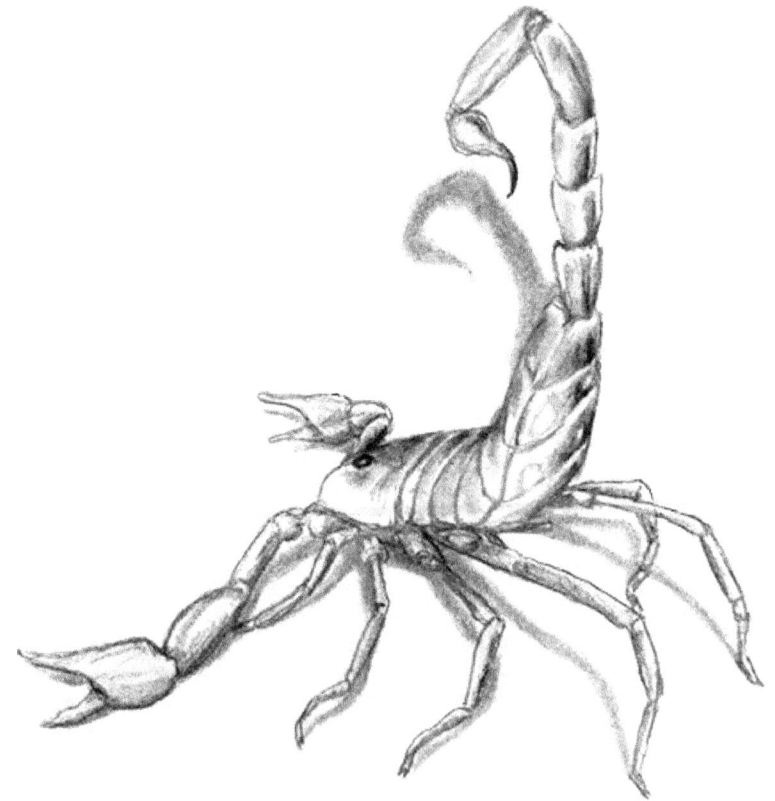

Foreshortening is necessary if the scorpion's body length (or the limbs) cannot be fully viewed on the chosen angle. The outline of the figure, thus, the shape, should be adjusted according to the view point. The modification in the length or the shape of any parts of the scorpion's figure can be easily adjusted and established if you would start with a base form (simple shapes and singular lines) before constructing the main outline of your drawing.

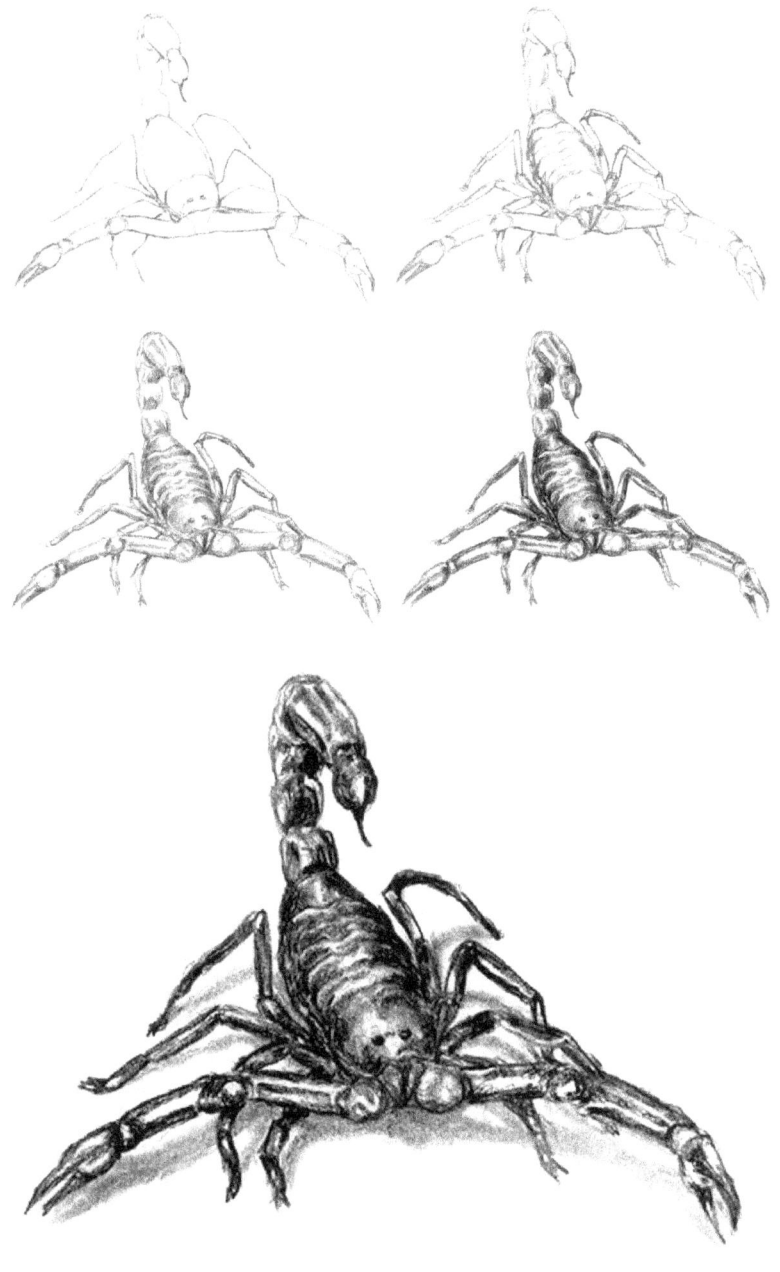

Black Emperor Scorpion

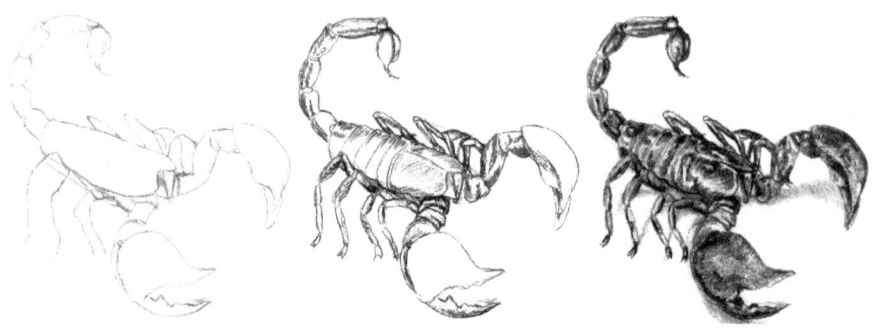

One of the most popular kind of scorpion is the black emperor scorpion or simply called emperor scorpion. Its significant size and gorgeous dark exoskeleton give it a strong and fierce appearance. Emperor scorpions are frequently used in movies; when in need of an icon or a symbol of deadly-looking crawler that could easily strike fear to people, it's probably an emperor scorpion. But despite of its intimidating look, the venom of emperor scorpion is non-fatal. It is known to be one of the largest kinds amongst the other types of scorpions, growing from 5 to 8 inches long. This breed is one of arachnid enthusiasts' favorite choice due to its calm nature and adaptive type of diet. If given enough space, one terrarium can be a home of two to three of its kind.

Emperor scorpions have big arms with bulky claws/pincers (this characteristic is said to distinguish and separate the scorpions with non-fatal venoms, to those that are deadly). The pincers have a rough surface. They are generally black (as the name says). Its dorsal side is glossy black with fairly wide back-armor (mesasoma), the tail is made with short and fairly thick caudal segments with a red stinger (telson). The sides of emperor scorpions are bright gray that is barely seen on the small gaps of its body armor. The intersegmental membranes (joints) are red to dark orange; the ventral side also contains the red-orange color value that can sometimes be apparent to the lower sides of the pincers and on the tips of its limbs.

Now, try this one using only your mere memory (or observation skill, if you have an image to base upon). Choose whatever kind of a scorpion's gesture you want and the angle or view that is easy for you.

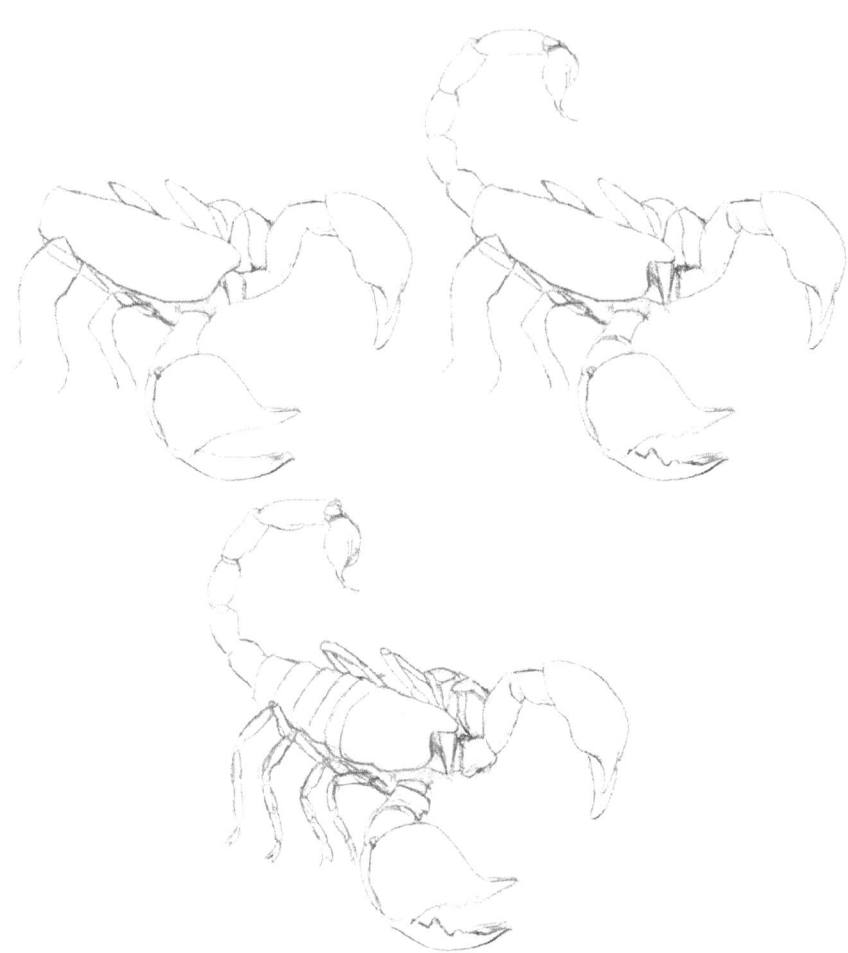

- Make a sketch of the scorpion's figure.

Pay no attention on the number of the segments of the abdomen or tail, nor the proper proportionate length or numbers of the segments of legs. Just simply make a sketch of a scorpion

The thing about an emperor scorpion is, most people who simply based on their memory of how they would describe a scorpion visually, such as being all black with fierce-looking pedipalps, is basically what this scorpion looks like. Drawing the arms with bulky pincers is enough for your idea of scorpion to be identified as an emperor scorpion.

- Apply some contour hatches.

Do not darken the drawing entirely, yet. Just put some hatches/parallel lines on the farther sides of your scorpion figure. And for describing the contour shape of the tail, apply two rows of hatches on each segment. shade the farther side of the tail segment, and then just put a little hatching to the side next to it, leaving the corner of the segment's shape unmarked (implying a highlight to this small portion). Do this same method to the legs and the arms. The idea is to make a separate shading on each different plane which constructs the figure of the scorpion entirely.

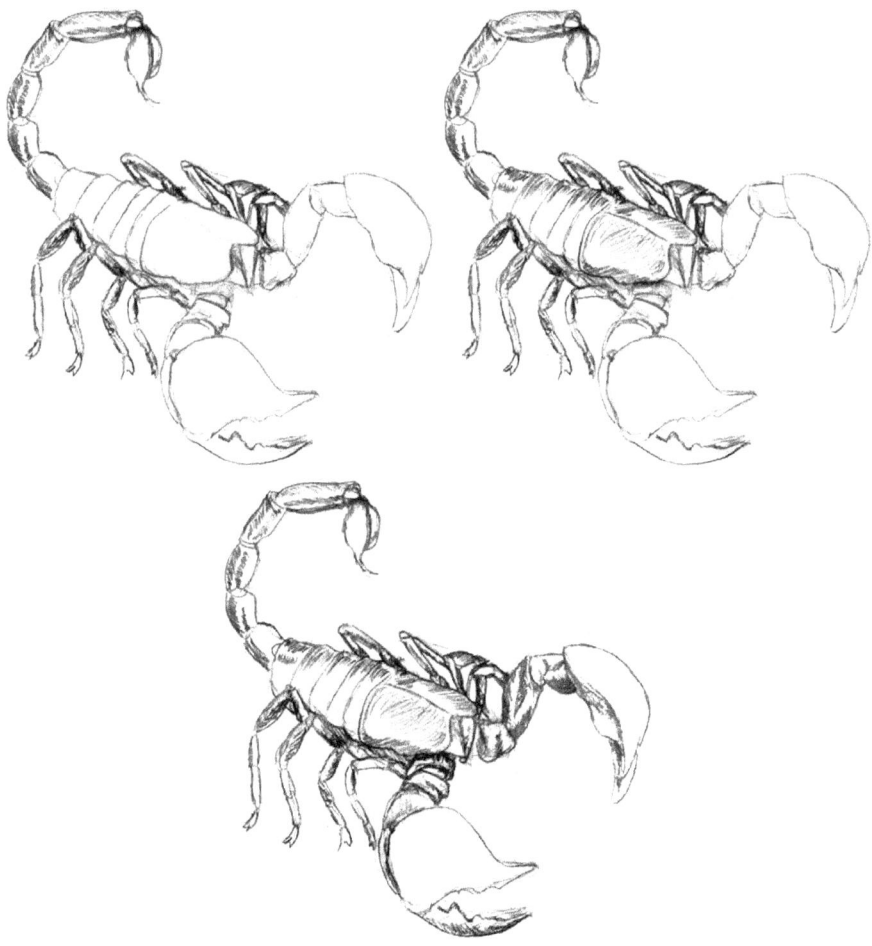

For the carapace or the head of the scorpion, make some arcing parallel lines. This would describe that plane is sloping and not entirely flat. And then shade the side of the carapace with thicker hatches, suggesting that this small plane is opposed to the direction of the light source. The same thing is applied to the entire figure. The thickness and lightness of the linear shading is adjusted based on its position from the source of light (which is at the top front of the scorpion, in this case).

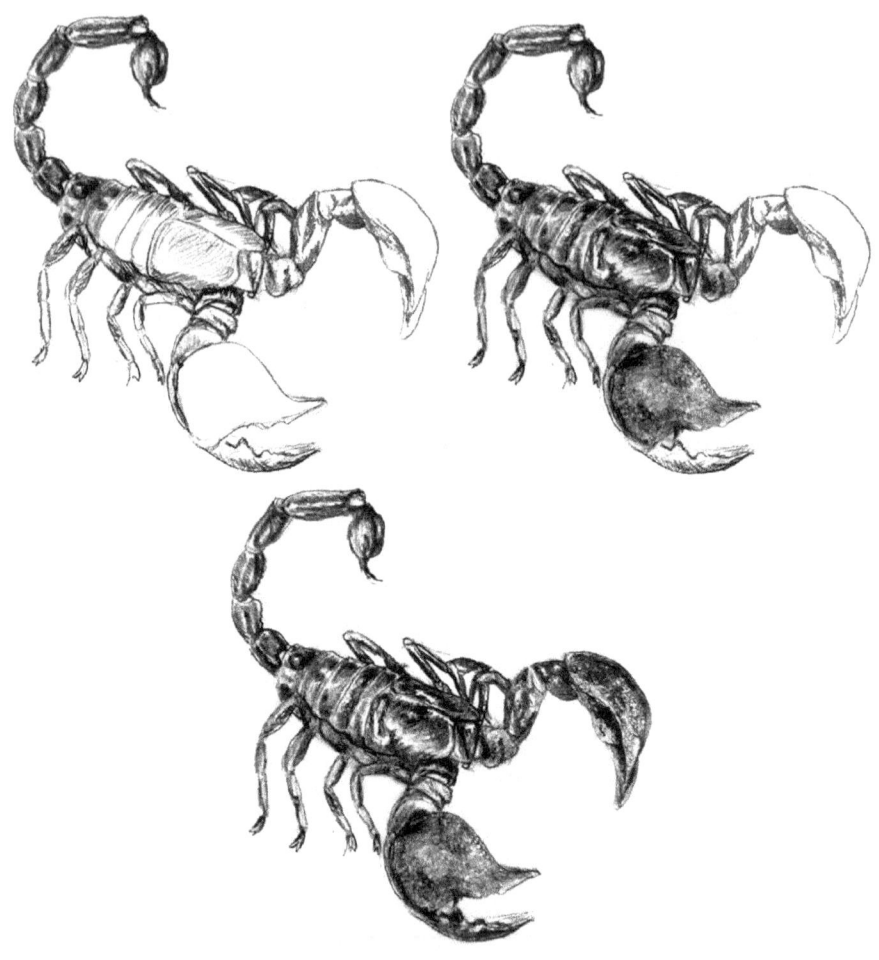

- Apply a thicker shading.

Now, darken the shades of your drawing. Applying another layer of hatches to your previously applied shades will naturally make the portion appear darker. Leave the subtle highlights unmarked; just overlap the area you shaded before.

For a gray tone, do not use hatches. Apply the shade on the other portions that should have a shade (remember that this should be a black scorpion) with small circular hand strokes or scribbles. Leave some edges of the outlines of the figure unmarked, mostly on the edges of the outlines on the nearer side.

To portray the rough texture of the pincers, do the same method of shading you used to achieve a gray tone. But this time, do it with heavier circular hand strokes. Make bigger (but not too big) scribbling strokes to make the circular lines more visible, creating subtle spaces on each circles you fill the area.

- Thicken the main outline.

Re-trace your main outline. The visibility of your main outline is probably overpowered by the darkest areas you shaded, so you have to thicken the lining to make it more visible.

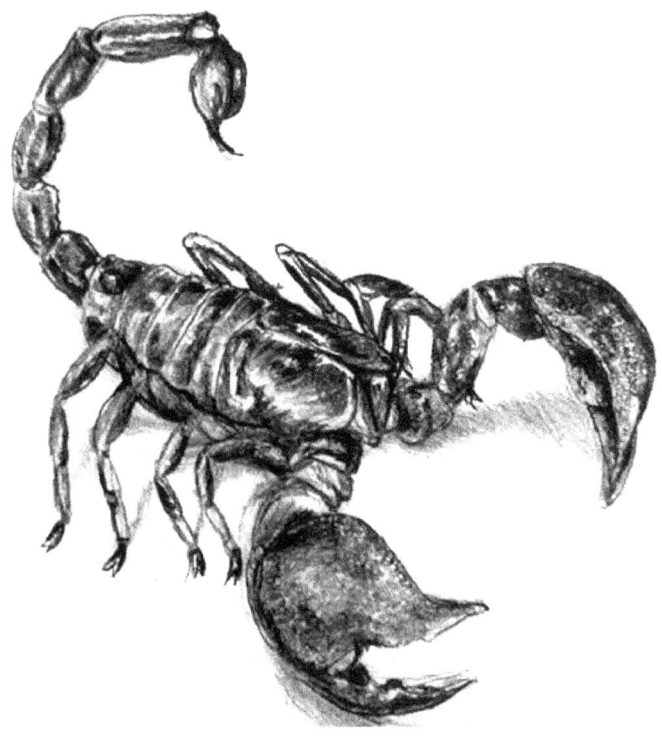

Striped Bark Scorpion

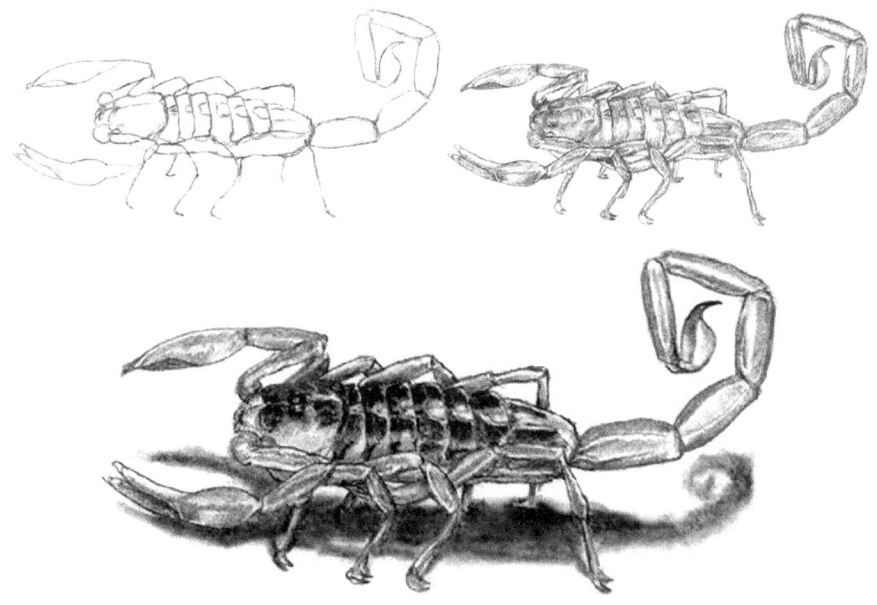

The striped bark scorpion is a small type of scorpion that can grow from 1 to 3 inches. It is also called the wood scorpion or a common striped scorpion. Unlike the other breeds (that is commonly seen on sand holes) this scorpion is usually found on cracks of trees and under flat rocks in the forest. In spite of its small size, striped bark scorpion is quite venomous.

The bodies of striped bark scorpions are generally yellow, having different shade values of the same color. The color tone ranges from dark to bright yellow, pale brown or faint copper tone. The arms (pincers) are slender and usually have a darker value compared to the other limbs (like pale brown pinchers matching a yellow body). The back (dorsal side) has the darkest color value, often in (depending on the climate of the scorpion's origin) black. On the dark-toned dorsal side of these scorpions are stripes of yellow to orange, vertical linings (one on each side and one at the middle) surrounding the body, they look like bars or patches of a brighter color rowed vertically (one on each segment of the tergate), contrasting the dark value of the scorpion's back-armor/exoskeleton.

- Draw the basic base figure.

Convey the figure of the scorpion in its simplest form using basic shapes and lines. You could use a long oval, a cylinder with sloping ends or anything that could be used to depict its semi-cylindrical body shape. Use a row of broken fairly long broken lines to establish the length of each tail segments, using a simple curve line might result into a tail having a segment that is too long or too short. The length of each line portraying the segments of the tail should get longer, from the base/oval and up to the stinger/telson.

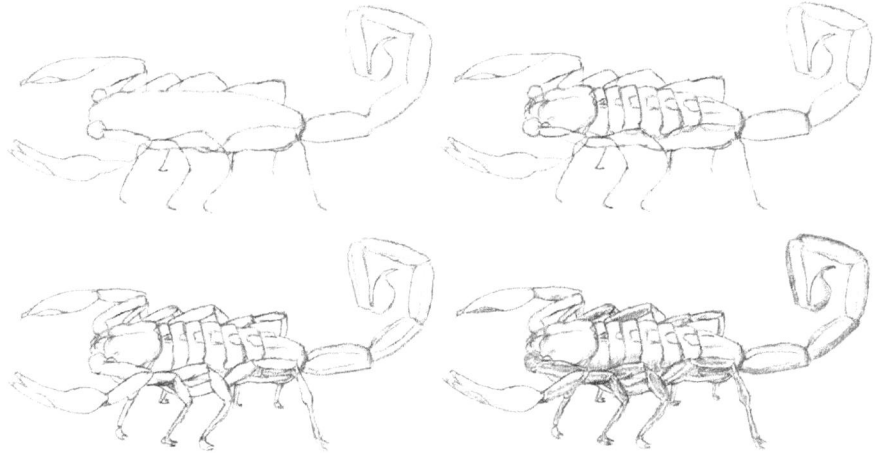

Use simple stick lines to establish the folds and length of each limb (the six legs and arms/palps).

- Construct the main outline.

Once you define the size and length of the base/body and the parts (legs, arms and tail), modify the line of the base (the oval or cylinder) and establish the thickness of the limbs and the tail.

The spaces between the segments of the tail should gradually increase as it reaches the tip.

The upper outline of the body has ridges due to the scorpion's abdominal segments. Draw 7 lines to establish the segments of the body, each line should curve with the dimensions of its semi-cylindrical contour shape. The first line would be the margining outline of the prosoma or the head, and the others would be the abdominal segments. Remember that the last segment should have more space (at least segment with a line gap that could equal to two previous segments) where the tail is connected.

At the middle of each abdominal segment, draw a rectangular/square patch, with the last segment having the longest one. This would be the 'stripe' of the stripe bark scorpion.

Draw the other linings included in the body; the slope and the horizontal lining on the carapace, and the segments of the legs and the arms.

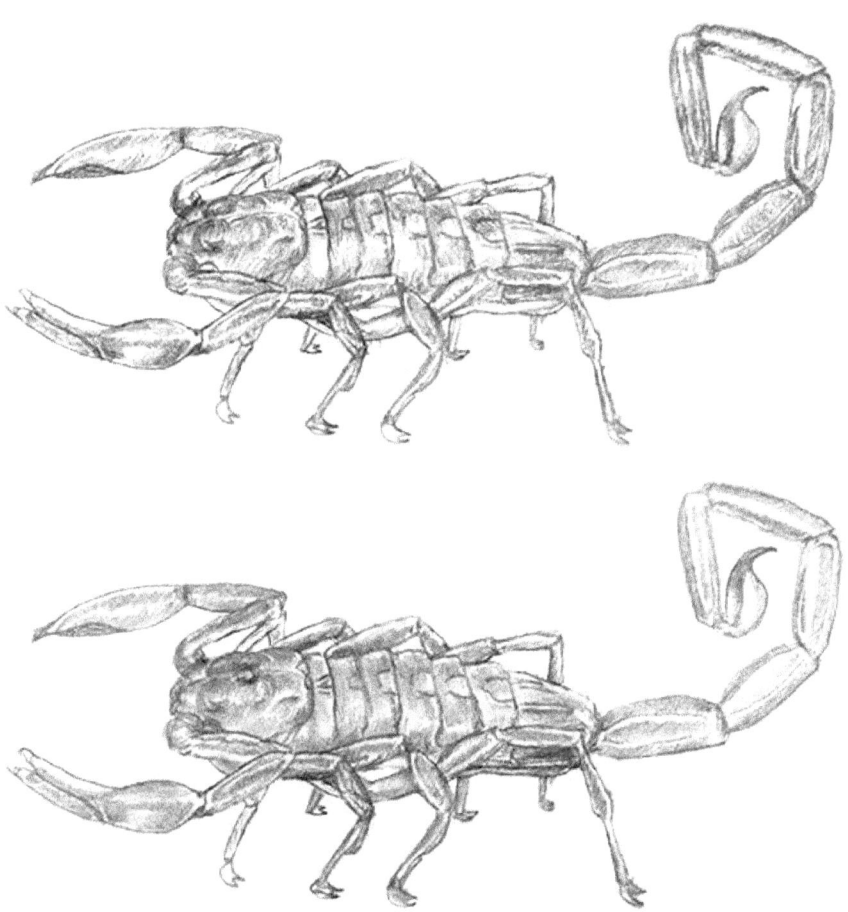

- Apply some linear shading.

Once the primary outline is established, begin portraying the figure's gradation/shades. The direction of the hatches should convey the planes of the figure. Use straight lines for the areas that are somehow flat, and use curving hatches for the areas with slopes. Leave some highlights on the side edges of the body parts to convey its texture.

- Smear the shades.

Smear the shades carefully. Do not randomly smudge the entire area with heavy hand strokes; smear each shading section by section. Take note of the highlights as you blur every linear shades you previously applied.

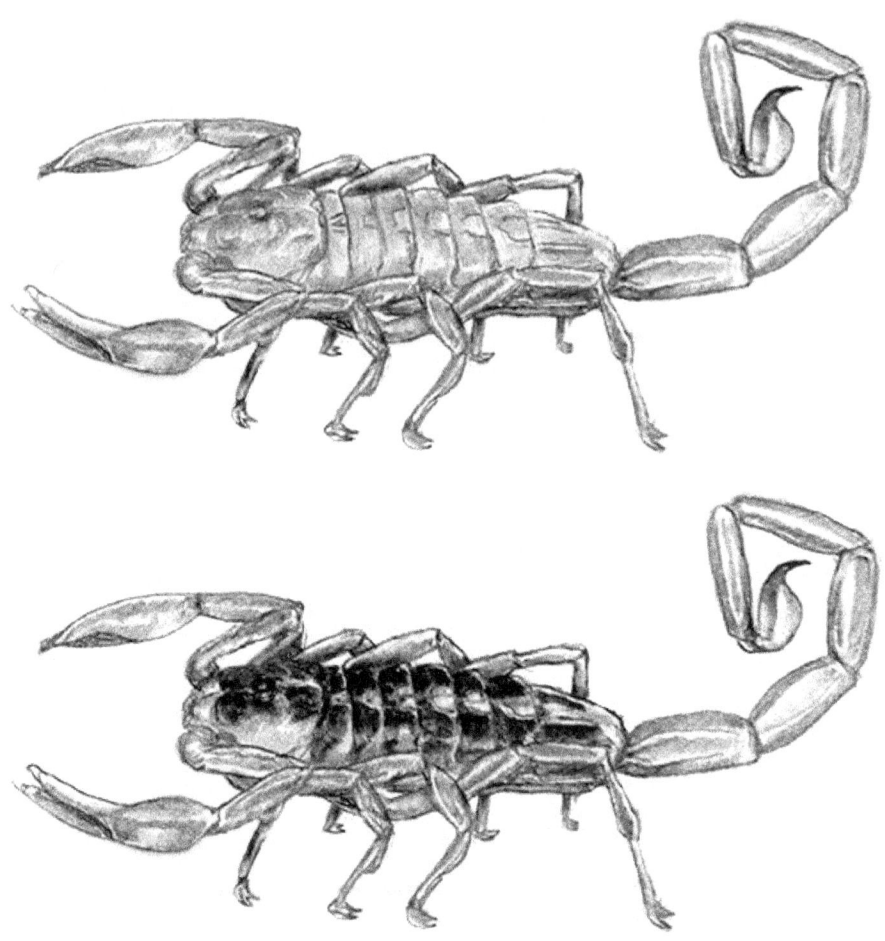

- Darken the back area of the scorpion.

Apply another layer of a darker shade at the back of the scorpion where the stripe lies. The darker value of its back would make the other shades appear brighter.

Regain the highlights by using a kneaded eraser. The stripe on it its back should have the brightest value, and the value of the gray tones should be adjusted according to the area it covers; for example, the upper side of the tail should be darker than the side at the front (in your viewpoint), but it should not be as dark as the shade at back of the scorpion, and the area with the lighter gray should not be as bright as the stripe marking.

- Re-define the blurred outlines.

Finalize the drawing by fixing the blurred outlines. It is much better to re-outline the entire figure once the shading process is complete.

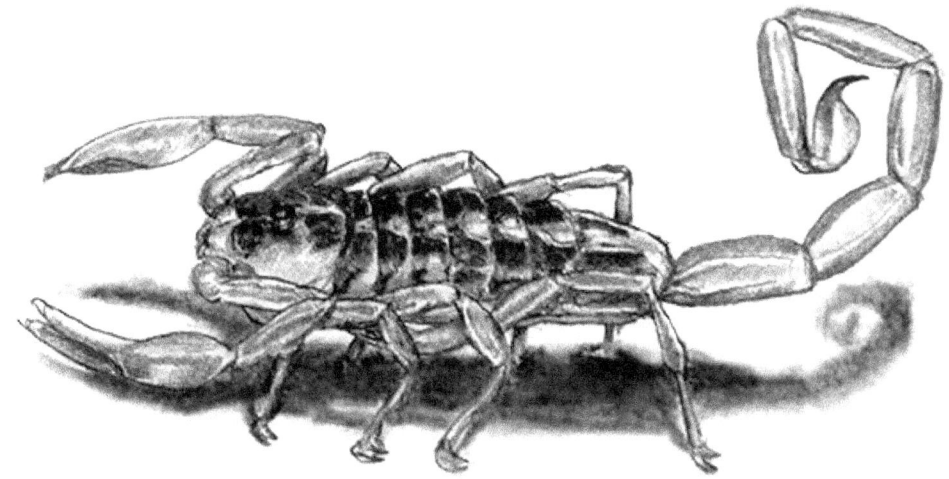

Amblypygi

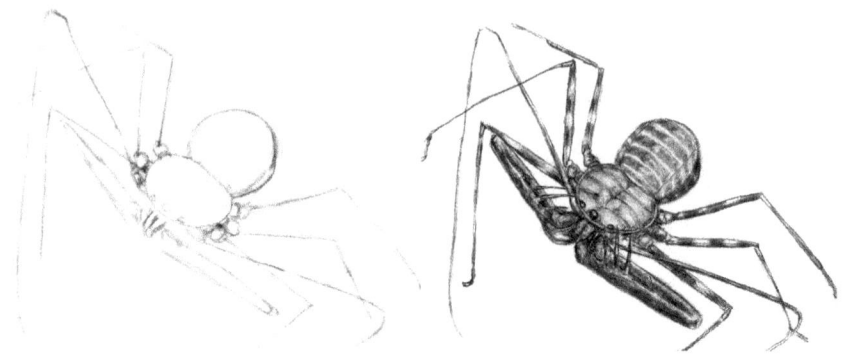

You probably recognize this one as the weird looking spider/ scorpion on one of the Harry Potter movies (when the curse spells are being demonstrated). The amblypygi is not specified as true scorpion (lacking the distinguishable tail of a scorpion, thus, non-deadly since it does not have a venom) and it is not recognized as a spider either, but it is definitely an arachnid. It is also called as the tailless whip scorpion or the whip spider. As an invertebrate that does not belong to the main breed/species of spider or scorpion, it is established as a different branch of the arachnid family. Amblypygi arachnids or amblypygids are the alter-kinds of the actual whip scorpions (vinegaroons) which is also a non-venomous type of the arachnid species. The name amblybygi means "flat-posterior".

Amblypygids (as the name describes) are flat, unlike the other species of arachnids which are semi-cylindrical in shape. They crawl sideways like a crab, especially when they are hunting for a food. In exchange to not having a venom to immobilize or stun a prey, their arms/pedipalps are strong enough to hold it down until it gives up on escaping, piercing it with the few thick spikes on their arm to have a good grasp and weaken it. And their jaws (chelicerae) are strong enough to snap off some of the prey's limb. They are basically poor-sighted, they use their significantly long first pair of legs (antenniform legs, having at least twice the length of the other legs) to locate their destination (in darkness) and find a potential target. The body of amblypygids can be compared to a spider's rather than a scorpion's; their carapace is flat round (disk-shaped), combined with a thick oval abdomen.

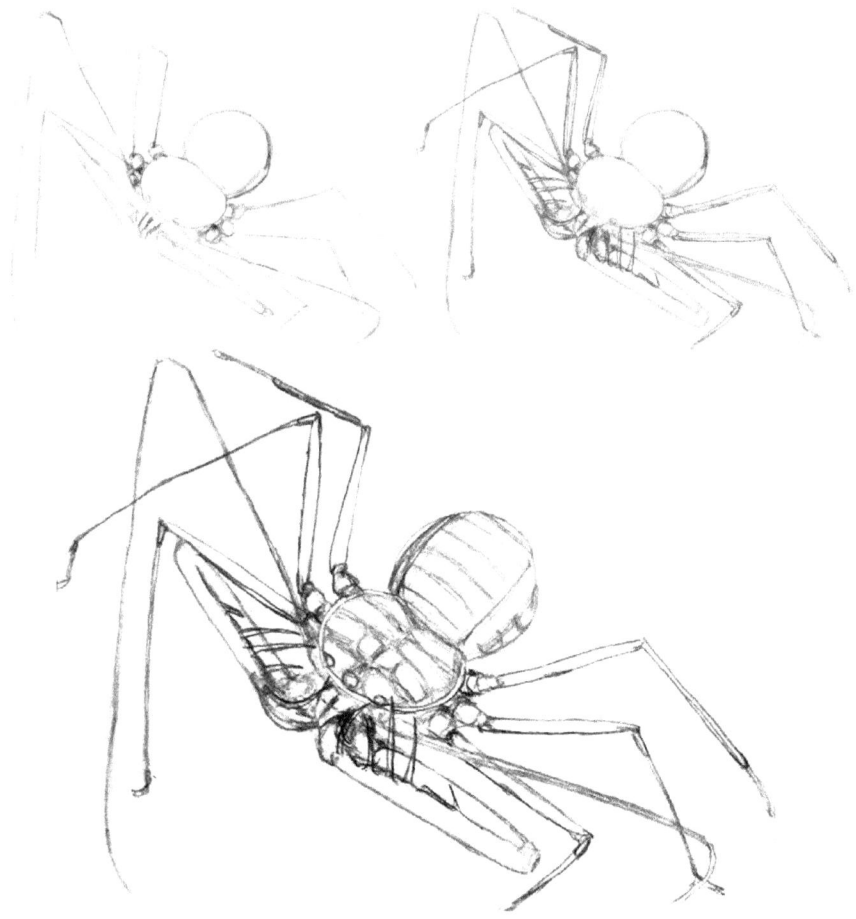

- Define the figure on its simplest form.

Draw a base first to easily construct a proper outline for your subject. Make two spheres as a base for the body. The sphere that represents the carapace should be somehow oblate. In an actual perfect top view, the carapace is actually more roundish than the abdomen, but due to my chosen view angle (upper side view), the carapace should be slightly foreshortened.

Use singular lines to easily establish the length of each limb; how they are positioned and how they folded. The whips or the antenniform legs should be significantly longer than the other limbs. The trochanter segment of amblypygis or the part of the leg that connects to the coxa (which connects the limbs to the body) is relatively bulkier compared to the other arachnids', they are somehow spherical instead of the usual cylindrical/tube shape.

- Establish the thickness of the limbs.

Convey the thickness of each limb. The first pair of legs (whips) should be thinner compared to the others. The first segment of the legs (femur to patella) is wider (but flattened) compare to the other segments next to the knees/patella.

The arms (having five to six spines) are thick (significantly thicker than the legs) and cylindrical, the spikes near the tip of the pedipalps are longer compared to the ones near the elbow.

- Draw the details of the body.

Once the main outline of the figure is constructed, erase the primary base and the other unnecessary line marks. Clean up the drawing and refine the outline to prepare it for detailing.

Although having a different form, the round abdomen of amblypygi also has seven segments. The spaces between each segments should be relatively even, having a margining outline on its round plane/surface. The carapace also has a subtle margin on its round disk-like shape, along with the subtle linings (one vertical and three horizontal, which are hardly noticeable) and minor slopes on its surface. The lateral eyes are somehow observable.

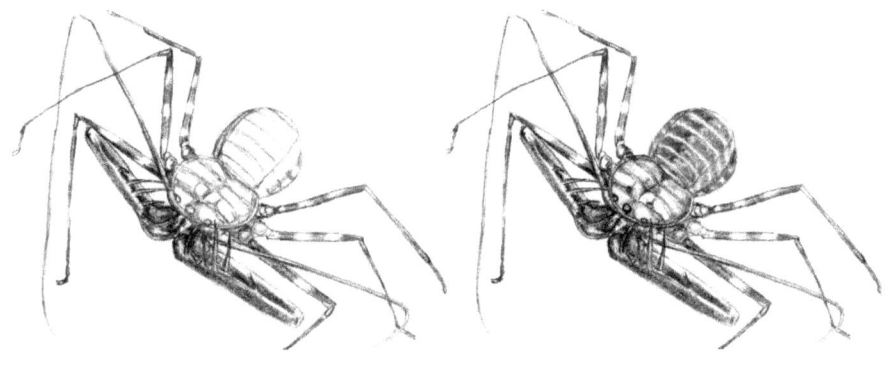

- Start applying the shades for establishing the body markings.

There are stripe markings all over its body. The legs have stripes and also the sides of the abdomen (aligned with the abdominal segments). But the pedipalps are simply dark toned and does not contain stripe markings. Use thin hatches for the stripes of the limbs, and then use scribbling strokes for the larger areas.

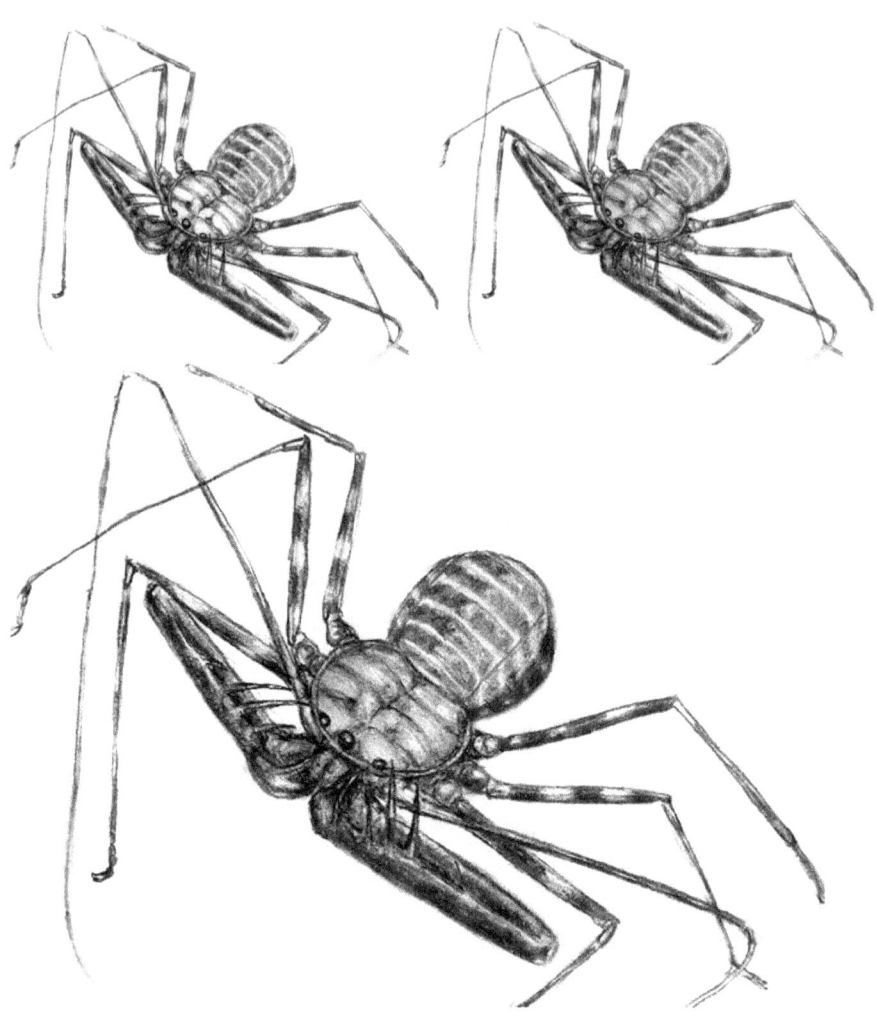

- Apply another layer of shade to establish dimensions.

Once the stripe markings are placed, smudge the shades with fairly light hand strokes (just enough to blur out the linear marks), and then apply another layer of shading to the areas that should appear darker (underneath the overlapped portions of the limbs, farther side of the abdomen, and the lower side of the dark-toned arms).

Apply a faint gray tone to the lower sides of the portions that are nearer and brighter (lower sides of the limbs, the carapace, nearer side of the abdomen). It is easier to apply a faint gray tone with just a used smudge stick.

- Finalize the drawing by re-darkening the darkest areas, and then re-define the main outline of the figure.

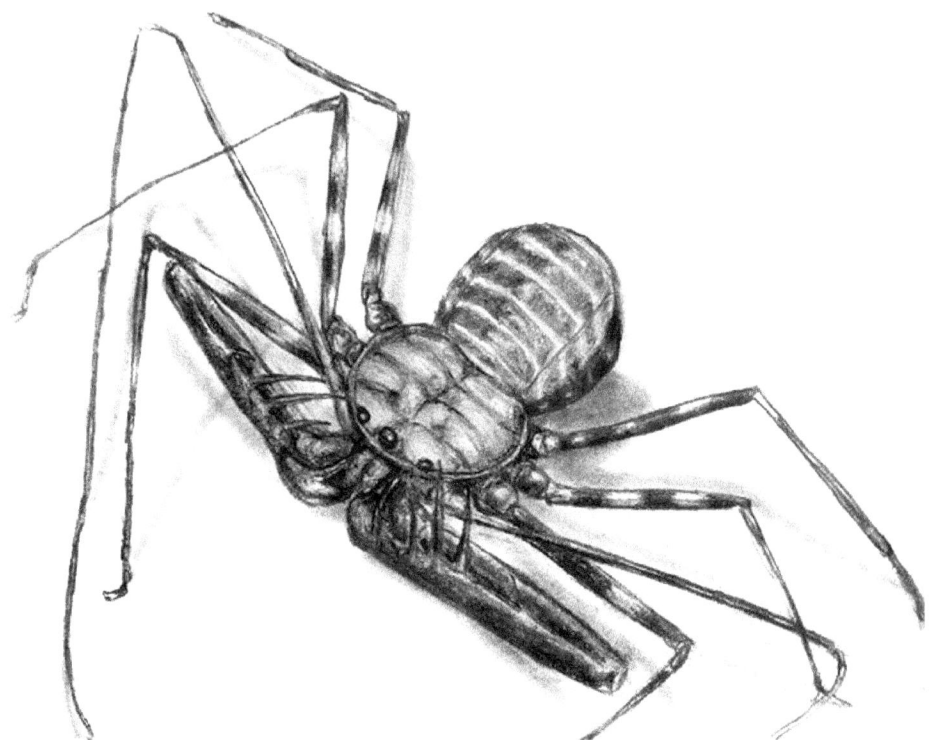

Whip scorpion

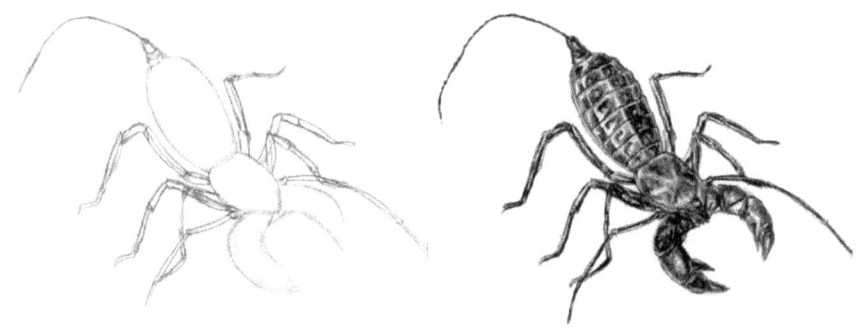

Uropygids or basically known as whip scorpions (or vinegaroons, also spelled as vinegarroons or vinegarones) are one of the unique breeds of the arachnid family. In spite of the name, they are not actual scorpions. They are undeniably related to them but are not categorized under scorpionida family. Uropygids are categorized simply as species of pedipalpi. The name was given because they have the physical features of actual scorpions, although they have whips for tails instead of stingers. The term uropygid is derived from a combination of two Greek words which means "tail rump". Excluding the tail and the limbs, their sizes can grow from 1 to 3 inches long. Whip scorpions are commonly found on tropical areas.

The appearance (shape and form) of a whip scorpion is basically like the real scorpion's, with few observable differences. The prosoma (upper portion is round and a little flat, while the opistosoma is oval, unlike the scorpion's slightly bean-shaped body (with prosoma and metasoma having the same marginal contour outline). Its arms are thick and fairly short; the whip-like telson (tail) has nearly the same length as the abdomen (opistosoma) or longer. The color of its exoskeleton ranges from deep brown to glossy black.

Whip scorpions are none venomous (due to the absence of venom glands), which is why they are often kept as pets. In exchange to not having a venom as a reliable way of self-defense, whip scorpions possess a gland (where the whip is connected) that produces acid (a combination of caprylic and acetic acid, having a vinegar-like odor; thus, the name vinegaroon) which they spray out to any potential threat/enemy if necessary.

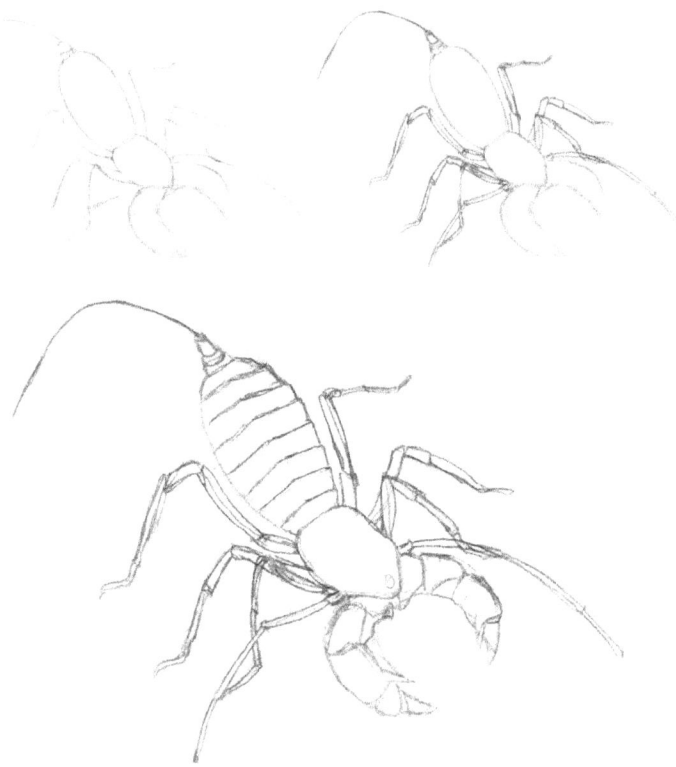

- Establish the size of the body and the length of the limbs.

Use an oval to establish the size of the abdomen. The length of the upper body is slightly smaller than the abdomen; the side connected to the abdomen is roundish while the head is triangular.

Establish the length and folds of each limb using stick/singular lines. The whips or the first pair of legs should be longer and are often curved at the front of the vinegaroon. And then establish the length of the whip-like tail. The robust arms are significantly thick and cylindrical. The first/non-movable claw of the pedipalp is relatively shorter compared to the other. The arms are usually in an arc gesture, forming a "C" shape.

- Draw the primary details.

Establish the thickness and the segments of each limb. Observe what portions of the limb overlap the other. The first pair of legs should be thinner compared to the others. Unlike the scorpions', a vinegaroon has 8 abdominal segments.

- Apply a thin layer of shading and convey the subtle details.

Each abdominal segment has a pair of dent (like a pair of dimples near the mid-area), and there are a subtle slopes near the edge of the abdomen's margin. Apply a faint shading to convey the subtle slopes and minor ridges of the body (on the abdomen and carapace) using thin and light hatches. Shade the sides of the pedipalps to convey the dimensions of its cylindrical shape. Also, apply some shade at the lower side of each leg.

- Smear the linear shading.

Smudge the shades to blur out the line markings of the hatches you previously applied. Take note of the highlights. Smear the shaded portions carefully and individually.

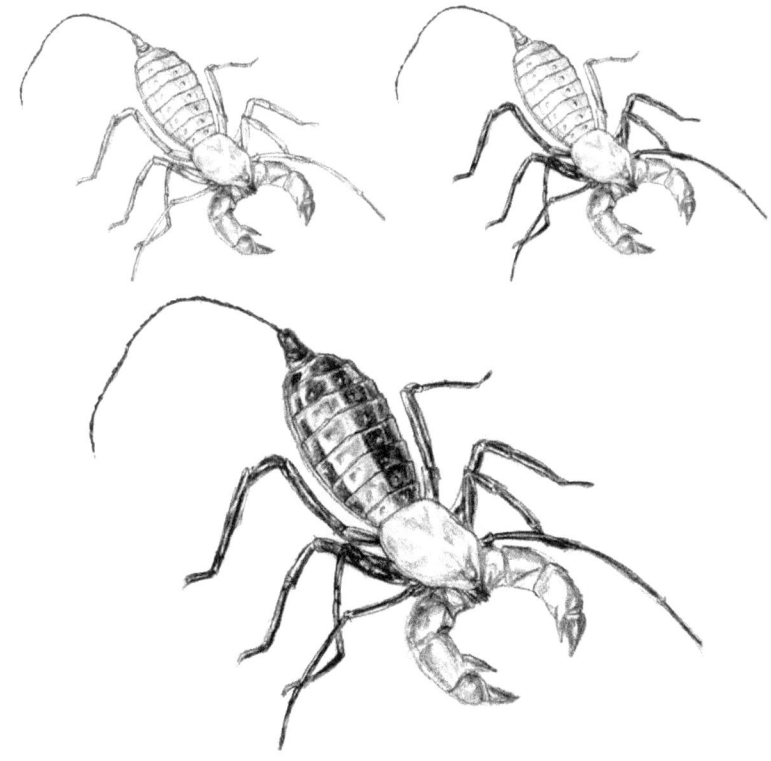

- Elaborate the gradation.

Apply another layer of shading. Darken the farther areas and the planes opposing the direction of light (simply base on the bright spots of the abdomen's subtle highlights to have am implied light source), such as the farther side of the abdominal segments and the right side of the left arm/pedipalp. Darken the portions of the limbs that are overlapped by the other. Thicken the shades on the lower sides of each limb and the

Subtle corners of the abdominal segments' dimples.

Finalize the drawing by re-defining the main outline of the vinegaroon's shape. And then cast a shadow underneath the figure. The shadow of the tail casted afar from the figure would portray that the abdomen is somehow raised from the ground. The distance between the shadows and the parts creating the shadow implies the distance between the figure and the surface it seats upon.

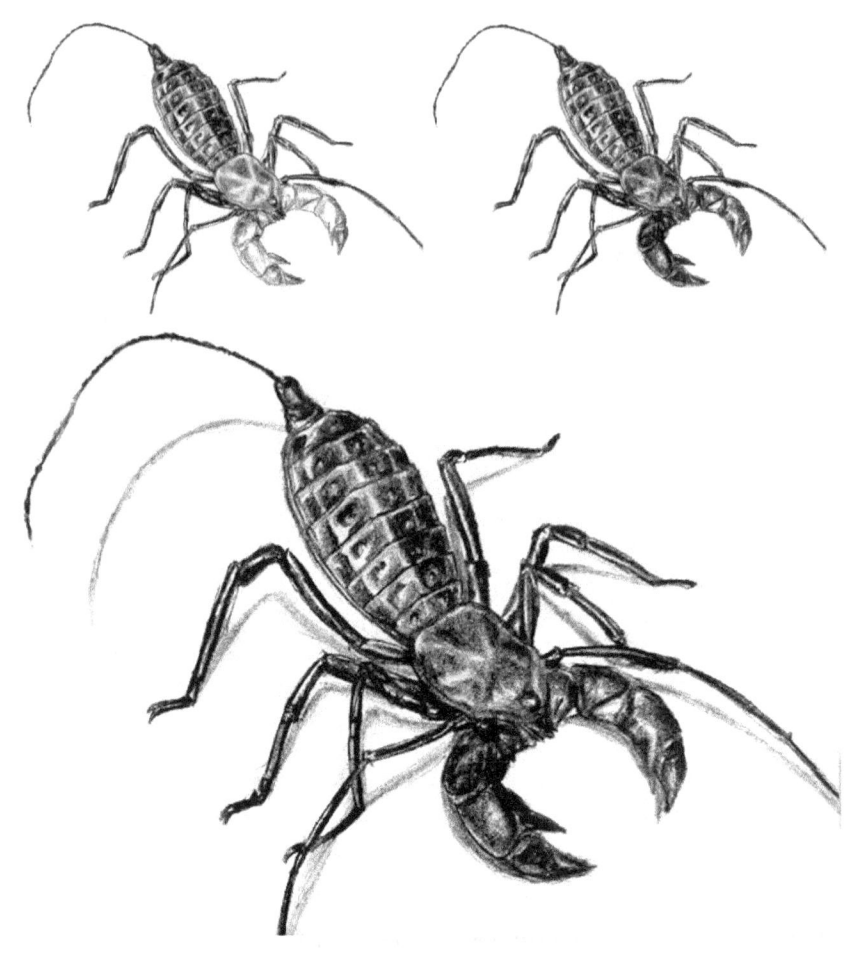

Thank you for reading.

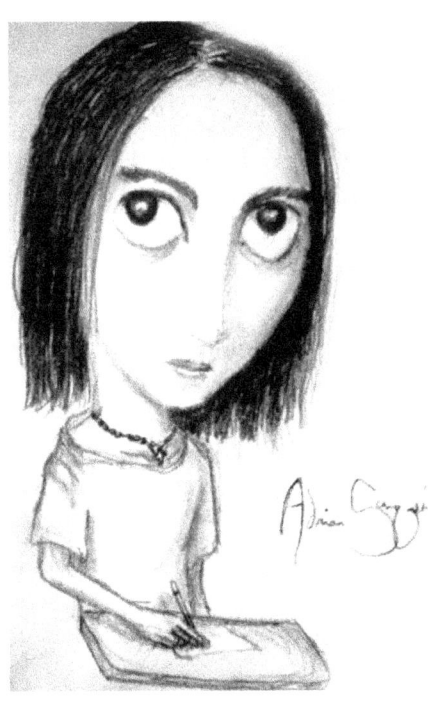

Author Bio

Check out some of my other books:

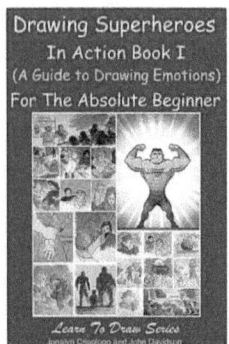

Drawing Superheroes In Action Book I (A Guide to Drawing Emotions) For The Absolute Beginner — Learn To Draw Series — Jonalyn Okeologo and John Davidson

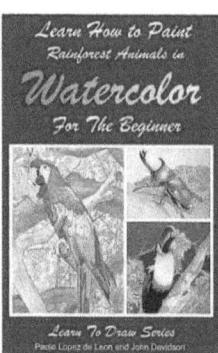

Learn How to Paint Rainforest Animals in Watercolor For The Beginner — Learn To Draw Series — Paolo Lopez de Leon and John Davidson

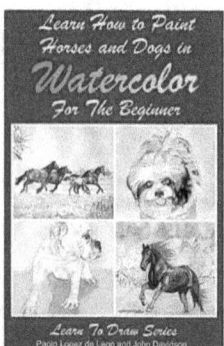

Learn How to Paint Horses and Dogs in Watercolor For The Beginner — Learn To Draw Series — Paolo Lopez de Leon and John Davidson

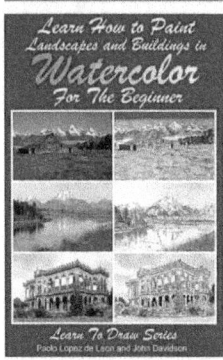

Learn How to Paint Landscapes and Buildings in Watercolor For The Beginner — Learn To Draw Series — Paolo Lopez de Leon and John Davidson

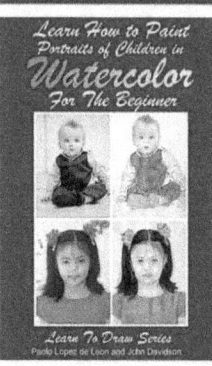

Learn How to Paint Portraits of Children in Watercolor For The Beginner — Learn To Draw Series — Paolo Lopez de Leon and John Davidson

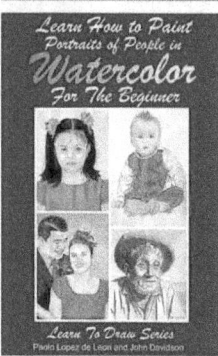

Learn How to Paint Portraits of People in Watercolor For The Beginner — Learn To Draw Series — Paolo Lopez de Leon and John Davidson

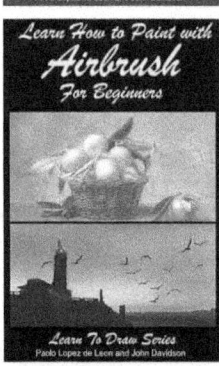

Learn How to Paint with Airbrush For Beginners — Learn To Draw Series — Paolo Lopez de Leon and John Davidson

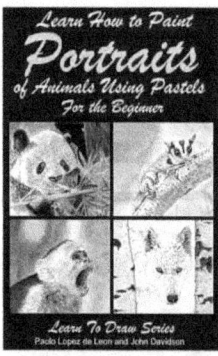

Learn How to Paint Portraits of Animals Using Pastels For the Beginner — Learn To Draw Series — Paolo Lopez de Leon and John Davidson

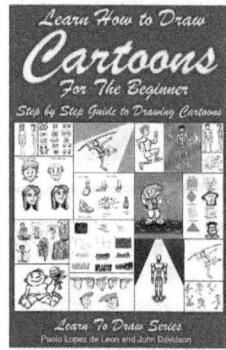

Learn How to Draw Cartoons For The Beginner Step by Step Guide to Drawing Cartoons — Learn To Draw Series — Paolo Lopez de Leon and John Davidson

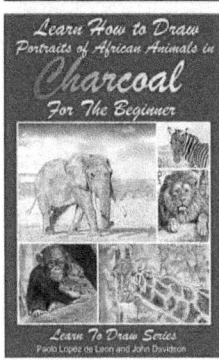

Learn How to Draw Portraits of African Animals in Charcoal For The Beginner — Learn To Draw Series — Paolo Lopez de Leon and John Davidson

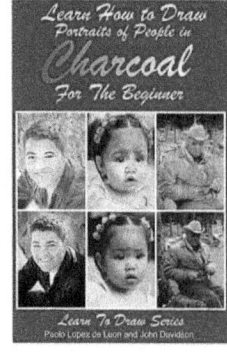

Learn How to Draw Portraits of People in Charcoal For The Beginner — Learn To Draw Series — Paolo Lopez de Leon and John Davidson

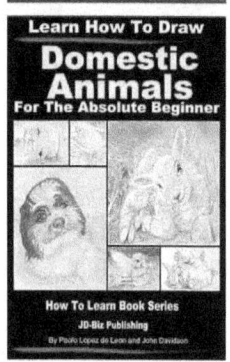

Learn How To Draw Domestic Animals For The Absolute Beginner — How To Learn Book Series — JD-Biz Publishing — By Paolo Lopez de Leon and John Davidson

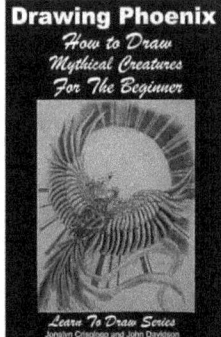

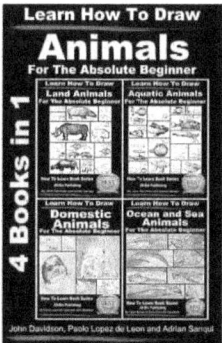

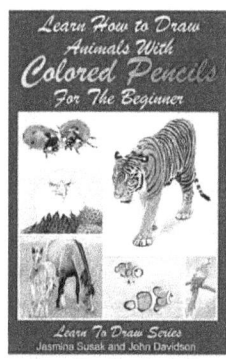

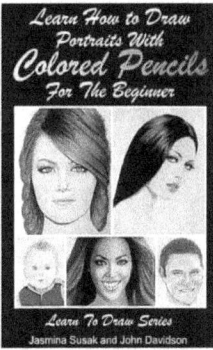

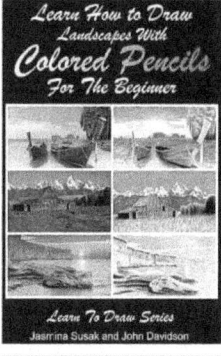

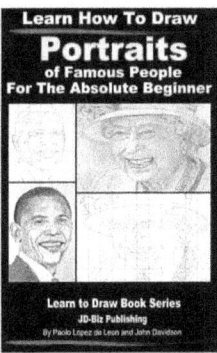

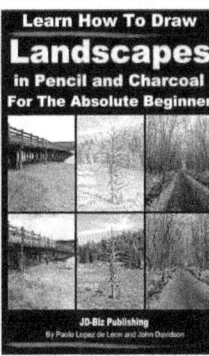

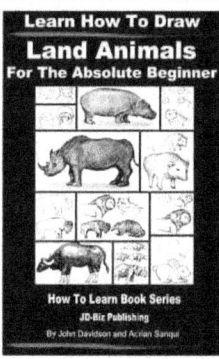

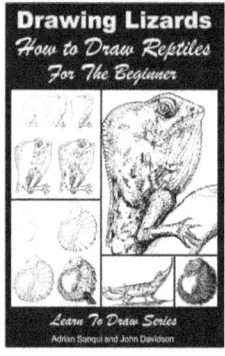

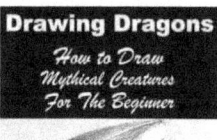

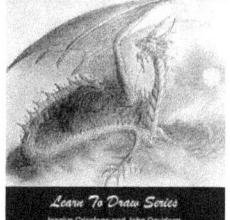

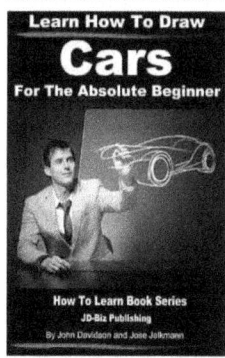

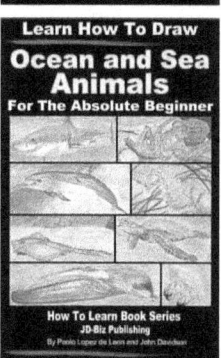

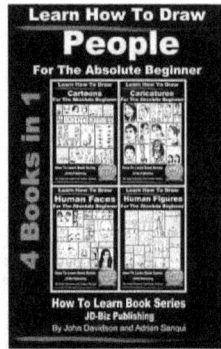

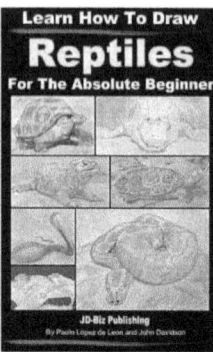

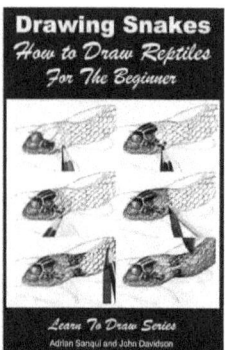

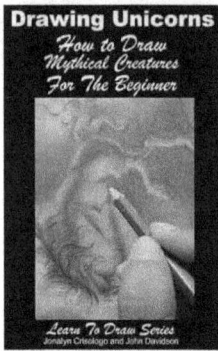

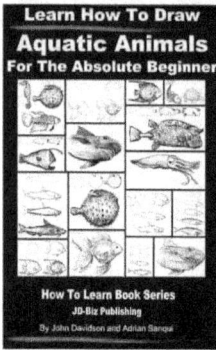

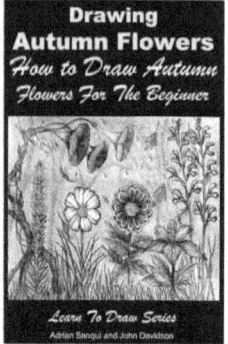

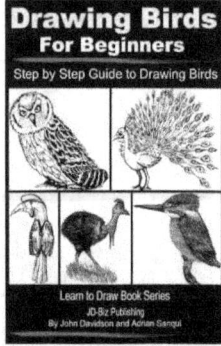

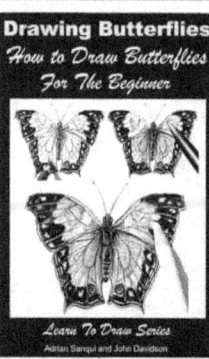

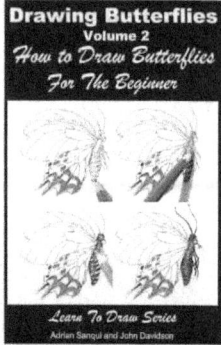

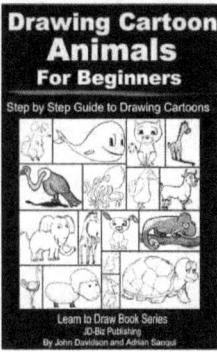

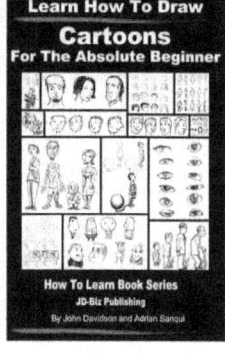

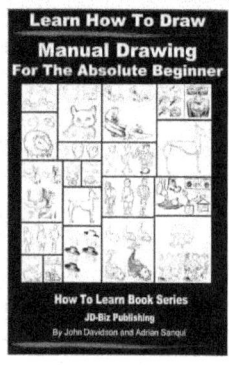

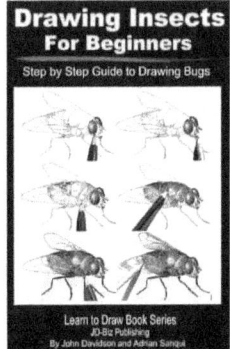

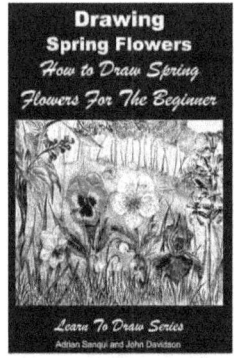

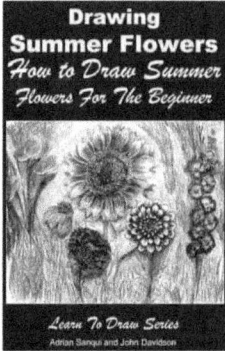

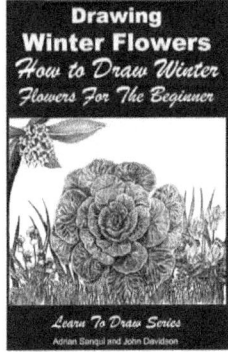

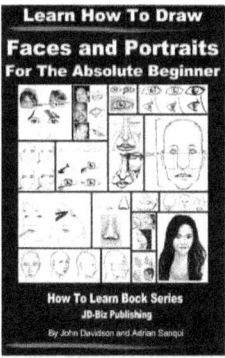

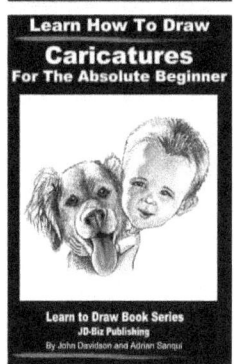

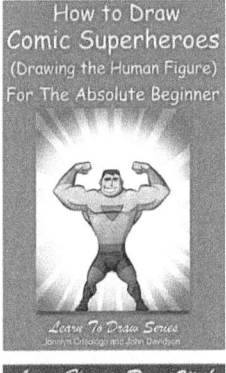

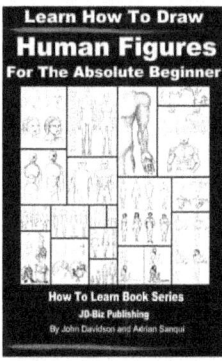

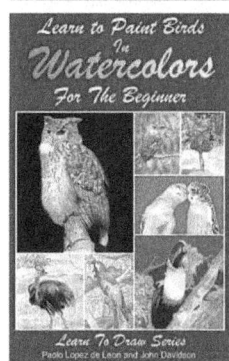

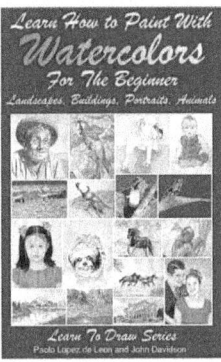

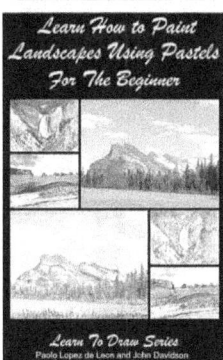

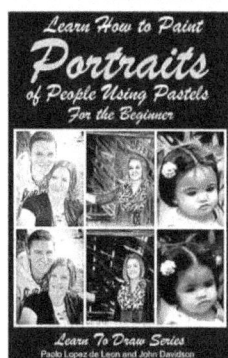

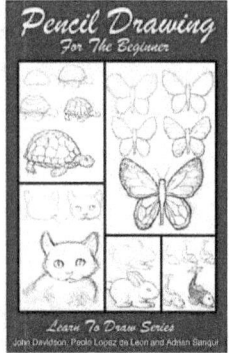

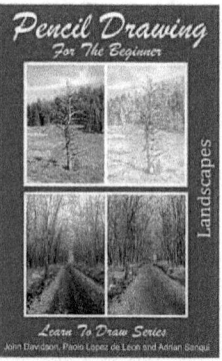

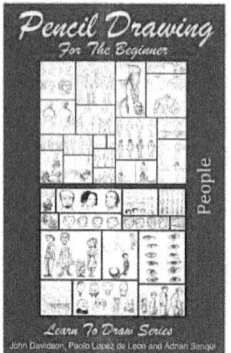

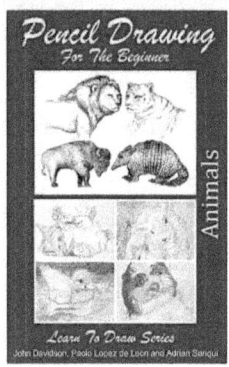

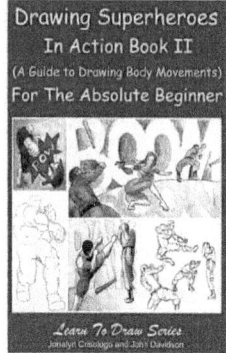

Publisher

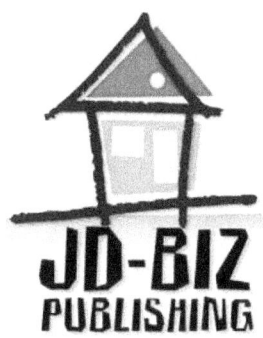

JD-Biz Corp

P O Box 374

Mendon, Utah 84325

http://www.jd-biz.com/

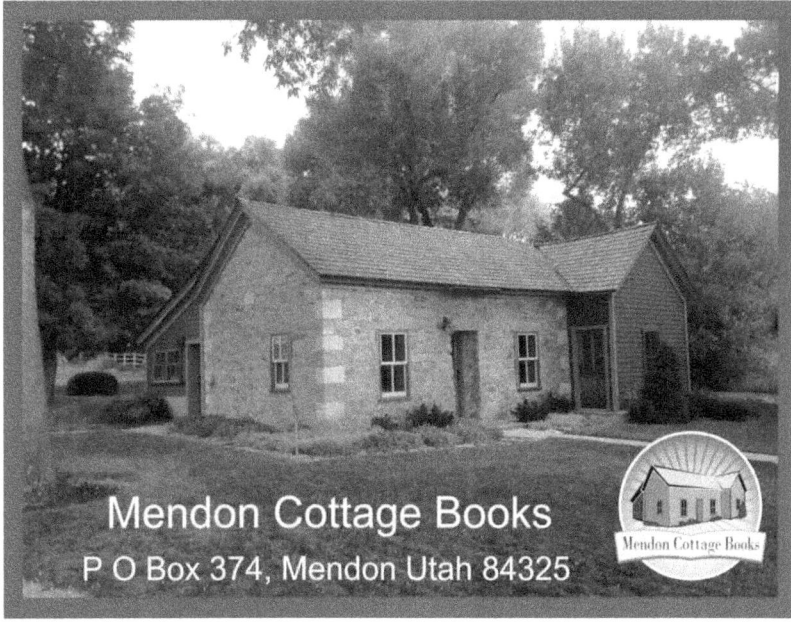

www.ingramcontent.com/pod-product-compliance
Lightning Source LLC
Chambersburg PA
CBHW071012180526
45168CB00003B/1397